THE
DECLARATION
of
INDEPENDENCE

with
SHORT BIOGRAPHIES
OF ITS SIGNERS

APPLEWOOD BOOKS
BEDFORD, MASSACHUSETTS

For information about this edition or for a free copy of our catalog of other Americana reprints, write to: Applewood Books, P.O. Box 365, Bedford, MA 01730.

ISBN 978-1-55709-448-3

Printed in the United States of America

10

Library of Congress Catalog Card Data: 96-30456

The *Declaration of Independence* was adopted by the Continental Congress July 4, 1776, and released to the public that day, signed only by John Hancock, president of the Congress. George Washington received his copy of the *Declaration* July 9 and had it read at six o'clock that evening to the troops encamped with him on York Island. The engravings and biographical information in this book come from B. J. Lossing's *Biographical Sketches of the Signers of the Declaration of American Independence*, published in 1848. Spelling and punctuation of the *Declaration* conform to the original document.

WHEN in the Course of human events, it becomes necessary for one people to dissolve the political bands which have connected them with another, and to assume among the powers of the earth, the separate and equal station to which the Laws of Nature and of Nature's God entitle them, a decent respect to the opinions of mankind requires that they should declare the causes which impel them to the separation.—

We hold these truths to be self-evident, that all men are created equal, that they are endowed by their Creator with certain unalienable Rights, that among these are Life, Liberty and the pursuit of Happiness.—

That to secure these rights, Governments are instituted among Men, deriving their just powers from the consent of the governed,—

That whenever any Form of Government becomes destructive of these ends, it is the Right of the People to alter or to abolish it, and to institute new Government, laying its foundation on such principles and organizing its powers in such form, as to them shall seem most likely to effect their Safety and Happiness. Prudence, indeed, will dictate that Governments long established should not be changed for light and transient causes; and accordingly all experience hath shewn, that man-kind are more disposed to suffer, while evils are sufferable, than to right themselves by abolishing the forms to which they are accustomed. But when a long train of abuses and usurpations, pursuing invariably the same Object evinces a design to reduce them under absolute Despotism, it is their right, it is their duty, to throw off such Government, and to provide new Guards for their future security.—

Such has been the patient sufferance of these Colonies; and such is now the necessity which constrains them to alter their former Systems of Government. The history of the present King of Great Britain is a history of repeated injuries and usurpations, all having in direct object the establishment of an absolute Tyranny over these States. To prove this, let Facts be submitted to a candid world.—

He has refused his Assent to Laws, the most wholesome and necessary for the public good.—

He has forbidden his Governors to pass Laws of immediate and pressing importance, unless suspended in their operation till his Assent should be obtained; and when so suspended, he has utterly neglected to attend to them.—

He has refused to pass other Laws for the accommodation of large districts of people, unless those people would relinquish the right of Representation in the Legislature, a right inestimable to them and formidable to tyrants only.—

He has called together legislative bodies at places unusual, uncomfortable, and distant from the depository of their public Records, for the sole purpose of fatiguing them into compliance with his measures. —

He has dissolved Representative Houses repeatedly, for opposing with manly firmness his invasions on the rights of the people.—

He has refused for a long time, after such dissolutions, to cause others to be elected; whereby the Legislative powers, incapable of Annihilation, have returned to the People at large for their exercise; the State remaining in the mean time exposed to all the dangers of invasion from without, and convulsions within.—

He has endeavoured to prevent the population of these States; for that purpose obstructing the Laws for Naturalization of Foreigners; refusing to pass others to encourage their migrations hither, and raising the conditions of new Appropriations of Lands.—

He has obstructed the Administration of Justice, by refusing his Assent to Laws for establishing Judiciary powers.—

He has made Judges dependent on his Will alone, for the tenure of their offices, and the amount and payment of their salaries.—

He has erected a multitude of New Offices, and sent hither swarms of Officers to harrass our people, and eat out their substance.—

He has kept among us, in times of peace, Standing Armies without the Consent of our legislatures.—

He has affected to render the Military independent of and superior to the Civil power.—

He has combined with others to subject us to a jurisdiction foreign to our constitution, and unacknowledged by our laws; giving his Assent to their Acts of pretended Legislation:—

For quartering large bodies of armed troops among us:—

For protecting them, by a mock Trial, from punishment for any Murders which they should commit on the Inhabitants of these States:—

For cutting off our Trade with all parts of the world:—

For imposing Taxes on us without our Consent:—

For depriving us in many cases, of the benefits of Trial by Jury:—

For transporting us beyond Seas to be tried for pretended offences:—

For abolishing the free System of English Laws in a neighbouring Province, establishing therein an Arbitrary government, and enlarging its Boundaries so as to render it at once an example and fit instrument for introducing the same absolute rule into these Colonies:—

For taking away our Charters, abolishing our most valuable laws, and altering fundamentally the Forms of our Governments:—

For suspending our own Legislatures, and declaring themselves invested with power to legislate for us in all cases whatsoever.—

He has abdicated Government here, by declaring us out of his Protection and waging War against us.—

He has plundered our seas, ravaged our Coasts, burnt our towns, and destroyed the lives of our people.—

He is at this time transporting large Armies of foreign Mercenaries to compleat the works of death, desolation and tyranny, already begun with circumstances of Cruelty & perfidy scarcely paralleled in the most barbarous ages, and totally unworthy the Head of a civilized nation.—

He has constrained our fellow Citizens taken Captive on the high Seas to bear Arms against their Country, to become the executioners of their friends and Brethren, or to fall themselves by their Hands.—

He has excited domestic insurrections amongst us, and has endeavoured to bring on the inhabitants of our frontiers, the merciless Indian Savages, whose known rule of warfare, is an undistinguished destruction, of all ages, sexes and conditions.

In every stage of these Oppressions We have Petitioned for Redress in the most humble terms: Our repeated Petitions have been answered only by repeated injury. A Prince, whose character is thus marked by every act which may define a Tyrant, is unfit to be the ruler of a free people.

Nor have We been wanting in attentions to our British brethren. We have warned them from time to time of attempts by their legislature to extend an unwarrantable jurisdiction over us. We have reminded them of the circumstances of our emigration and settlement here. We have appealed to their native justice and magnanimity, and we have conjured them by the ties of our common kindred to disavow these usurpations, which, would inevitably interrupt our connections and correspondence. They too have been deaf to the voice of justice and of consanguinity. We must, therefore, acquiesce in the necessity, which denounces our Separation, and hold them, as we hold the rest of mankind, Enemies in War, in Peace Friends.—

We, therefore, the Representatives of the united States of America, in General Congress, Assembled, appealing to the Supreme Judge of the world for the rectitude of our intentions, do, in the Name, and by Authority of the good People of these

Colonies, solemnly publish and declare, That these United Colonies are, and of Right ought to be Free and Independent States; that they are Absolved from all Allegiance to the British Crown, and that all political connection between them and the State of Great Britain, is and ought to be totally dissolved; and that as Free and Independent States, they have full Power to levy War, conclude Peace, contract Alliances, establish Commerce, and to do all other Acts and Things which Independent States may of right do.—

And for the support of this Declaration, with a firm reliance on the protection of divine Providence, we mutually pledge to each other our Lives, our Fortunes, and our sacred Honor.

THE SIGNERS

In June of 1776, a committee was commissioned to draft a Declaration of Independence. "This committee consisted of Thomas Jefferson, John Adams, Benjamin Franklin, Roger Sherman, and Robert R. Livingston. The draft was made by Jefferson, and after a few verbal alterations by Dr. Franklin and Mr. Adams, it was submitted to Congress on the twenty-eighth of June." On the first of July, nine states voted for independence. On the fourth of July, the thirteen united Colonies declared themselves free and independent States. John Hancock, the president of Congress, was the only one to sign it that day. It was released to the world with only his signature, but on August 2, 1776, all but one of the 56 signers put their pens to the parchment. Matthew Thornton, the lone absentee, did not sign until November.

JOSIAH BARTLETT (1729–1795). A doctor, he was elected to the provincial legislature of New Hampshire in 1765 but turned against the British when the Stamp Act was passed. He served as a member of the Continental Congress from 1774 to 1778, was appointed chief justice of his state's Court of Common Pleas in 1779, and elected the first governor of New Hampshire in 1793 under the new federal Constitution.

Josiah Bartlett

WILLIAM WHIPPLE (1730–1785). Elected a member of the Continental Congress in 1776, he resigned from Congress in 1777, having been appointed a brigadier general of the New Hampshire Militia. He recruited and equipped troops, then led a brigade against Burgoyne and was serving under General Gates when Burgoyne was captured. He acted as a judge and federal commissioner from 1782 to 1785.

Wm Whipple

MATTHEW THORNTON (1714–1803). An advocate of colonists' rights from the middle of the century on, he was appointed a delegate to the Continental Congress in September 1776, and was allowed to sign the Declaration of Independence when he took his seat in November, four months after its publication. Thornton left Congress in 1778 and resumed his duties as a judge of the New Hampshire Superior Court. He resigned in 1782.

Matthew Thornton

JOHN HANCOCK (1737–1793). A symbol of open resistance to British rule even before the Boston Massacre of 1770, he became president of the Continental Congress in 1775 and released the Declaration of Independence July 4, 1776, his bold signature the only one on the document. The first elected governor of Massachusetts, Hancock was instrumental in getting his state to ratify the new U.S. Constitution in 1788.

ROBERT TREAT PAINE (1731–1814). Elected a member of the Provincial Assembly in 1773 and a member of the General Congress in 1774, he left Congress in 1777 to become attorney general of Massachusetts. He helped frame the state Constitution, adopted in 1780. Appointed a Supreme Court judge in 1790, he served in that capacity until he retired in 1804.

ELBRIDGE GERRY (1744–1814). Active in Massachusetts politics, he was a member of the Provincial Congress at the time of the battle of Bunker Hill. Elected to the Continental Congress in 1776, he retired in 1780, was reelected in 1783, and retired again in 1785. He served as a U.S. congressman, 1789–93, and as governor, 1810–11. In 1811, he became vice president of the United States under James Madison and died in office.

JOHN ADAMS (1735–1826). A lawyer, he was chosen as a representative to the Provincial Assembly in 1770, the same year he successfully defended the British soldiers involved in the Boston Massacre. Elected to the first Continental Congress in 1774, in 1776 he helped draft the Declaration of Independence. Adams served two terms as vice president under George Washington, then was elected second President of the United States. He and Jefferson passed away the same day, July 4, 1826.

John Adams

SAMUEL ADAMS (1722–1803). He began agitating for independence in 1763, and was elected to the General Assembly in 1765 and the Colonial Congress in 1766. A loud and visible spokesman for freedom, only he and John Hancock were excluded from the general pardon offered the rebellious patriots in 1775. Elected to the Continental Congress in 1774, he retired from Congress in 1781.

Sam'l Adams

STEPHEN HOPKINS (1707–1785). Elected governor of Rhode Island in 1756, he became an early opponent of the repressive British policies. In 1774, while chief justice of Rhode Island, he was elected to the Continental Congress. He served on the committee that drafted the Articles of Confederation in 1778. Opposed to slavery, he freed his own slaves in 1774.

Step. Hopkins

WILLIAM ELLERY (1727–1820). A successful lawyer, Ellery so infuriated the British with his patriotic activities that they burned his home and destroyed most of his property when they took Newport. He served as a Rhode Island Supreme Court justice. *William Ellery* After the U.S. Constitution was adopted in 1788, he was appointed collector for the port of Newport, and retained that position the rest of his life.

C O N N E C T I C U T

ROGER SHERMAN (1721–1793). Self-educated, he became a lawyer and a judge. Politically active in Connecticut from 1755, he was elected to the Continental Congress in 1774. He was appointed to the committee to prepare a draft of the *Roger Sherman* Declaration of Independence, and remained in Congress throughout the war. A delegate to the Constitutional Convention of 1787, he then served in the U.S. House (1789–91) and U.S. Senate (1791–93).

SAMUEL HUNTINGTON (1732–1796). Another self-taught lawyer, he was elected to the General Assembly of Connecticut in 1764, appointed a Superior Court judge in 1774, and delegated to the Continental Congress in 1775. He succeeded John  Jay as president of Congress in 1779 *Sam" Huntington* and served in that capacity until 1781. In 1785 he became lieutenant governor of Connecticut, moved up to governor the following year, and died while still in office.

WILLIAM WILLIAMS (1731–1811). Williams held a seat in the Connecticut Assembly for 45 years and was elected to the General Congress in 1775. He fought in the Connecticut militia during the Revolutionary War and spent his own money to further the war effort. He retired from politics in 1804.

OLIVER WOLCOTT (1726–1797). Delegated to the second General Congress in 1775, he returned to Connecticut after signing the Declaration and took command of 14 militia regiments. He served throughout the Revolutionary War, recruiting and leading troops as needed. He helped General Gates defeat Burgoyne at Saratoga in 1777, successfully defended the southwestern coast of Connecticut in 1779, and remained militarily active until 1783. He was lieutenant governor of Connecticut 1787–96, and governor 1796–97.

NEW YORK

WILLIAM FLOYD (1734–1821). First elected to Congress in 1774, he also engaged in military exercises as commander of the militia of Suffolk County in New York. British troops occupied his mansion and estate for seven years while he served in federal Congress and in the state senate. He was elected to the first Congress to convene under the new Constitution in 1789, and continued in various public offices until his death.

PHILIP LIVINGSTON (1716–1778). He began his public career in 1754 as alderman of the East Ward of New York City. Elected to the first Continental Congress in 1774 and to the first New York Senate in 1777, he died in 1778 while Congress was in session.

Phil. Livingston

FRANCIS LEWIS (1713–1803). A wealthy businessman, he represented New York at the Colonial Congress of 1765 and served in the Continental Congress 1774–79. When the British captured Long Island, his property was destroyed and his wife taken prisoner and confined for several months.

Fran'. Lewis

LEWIS MORRIS (1726–1798). First elected to the Continental Congress in 1775, Morris signed the Declaration even though he knew he risked losing his vast wealth and possessions. His brother, Gouverneur Morris, succeeded him in Congress in 1777.

Lewis Morris

NEW JERSEY

RICHARD STOCKTON (1730–1781). He joined the New Jersey Supreme Court in 1774 and was elected to the General Congress in 1776. Captured by the British, he was treated harshly for having signed the Declaration of Independence and lost his health as well as his wealth.

Rich'. Stockton

JOHN WITHERSPOON (1722–1794). He emigrated to America in 1768 to take over as president of New Jersey College (now Princeton University). Elected to the General Congress in 1776, he served on many of the most important committees until 1782.

FRANCIS HOPKINSON (1737–1791). He served as New Jersey delegate to the General Congress in 1776 and loan commissioner for a number of years. After officiating as judge of admiralty for Pennsylvania, he was appointed district judge of that state by President Washington in 1790.

JOHN HART (1714–1780). Active in promoting freedom since 1765, he was elected to the first Continental Congress in 1774. He retired in 1775 to tend to his estate, but served as vice president of the Provincial Congress of New Jersey. A delegate to the General Congress in 1776, he lost everything when the British overran New Jersey.

ABRAHAM CLARK (1726–1794). Elected to the Continental Congress in 1776, he remained in Congress until the war ended in 1783. His two sons were incarcerated by the British on the prison ship *Jersey*. Politically active, in 1788 he was elected to the first Congress under the new Constitution.

ROBERT MORRIS (1733–1806). A successful Philadelphia businessman, he was elected to the General Congress in 1775 and immediately took over finances. When the United States could not obtain credit, he personally secured the financing necessary to continue and complete the Revolutionary War.

In 1781 Morris established a creditable banking system in Philadelphia and was appointed by Congress the first secretary of the treasury. A delegate to the Constitutional Convention, he was elected a senator to the first U.S. Congress and retired after one full term.

BENJAMIN RUSH (1745–1813). Rush began championing the cause of freedom in 1768 and was elected to Congress in 1776. He was appointed physician general of the military hospitals by Congress in 1777 and served as president of the mint 1788–1802. A distinguished author, professor, and physician, he attracted thousands of students from the United States and Europe to his lectures in Philadelphia.

JOHN MORTON (1724–1777). A member of the General Assembly of Pennsylvania, he was a delegate to the Stamp Act Congress in 1765. He was appointed a delegate to the General Congress in 1774, 1775, and 1776 and cast the deciding vote in favor of independence.

JAMES SMITH (1720–1806). In 1774 he raised and drilled the first volunteer militia at York, where he resided. He was active in creating a state Constitution for Pennsylvania. During the Revolutionary War he was a member of the team advising and superintending all military operations. He remained in Congress until 1778, then went to the state legislature for a year.

BENJAMIN FRANKLIN (1706–1790). Inventor, statesman, philosopher, and military tactician, Dr. Franklin represented Pennsylvania in London as early as 1757. In England when the Stamp Act was passed in 1765, he returned to the Colonies in 1775 and was elected to the General Congress that year and the next. He helped draft the Declaration of Independence. Though over 70, he returned to France in 1776 and negotiated a treaty of alliance in 1778. France acknowledged America's independence and pledged military and financial aid. Franklin signed the peace treaty with England in 1783 but did not return home until 1785.

GEORGE TAYLOR (1716–1781). A member of the Colonial Assembly in 1764, he was elected to the Provincial Congress in 1775. He was appointed to the General Congress in 1776 and remained in Congress one year.

GEORGE CLYMER (1739–1813). Very active in organizing resistance to the British in Philadelphia before the Revolutionary War, he was appointed to the General Congress in 1776, and remained a member of Congress until 1783. During the Revolutionary War he negotiated treaties with the Indians in western Pennsylvania to stop attacks on settlers there, and after the war helped Robert Morris set up a national bank in Philadelphia.

JAMES WILSON (1742–1798). He was elected to the Provincial Assembly in 1774 and to the General Congress from 1775 to 1777 and from 1783 to 1787. He helped frame the U.S. Constitution and chaired the committee that reported the first draft. Appointed to the U.S. Supreme Court by President Washington in 1789, he also served as a judge of the U.S. Supreme Circuit Court and died while on a judicial circuit in North Carolina.

GEORGE ROSS (1730–1780). One of seven delegates from Pennsylvania to the first General Congress in 1774, he remained in Congress until 1777. A peacemaker as well as a patriot, Ross sought justice for the Indian tribes in his state and helped negotiate peace treaties with them. He also defended the rights of despised Tories.

GEORGE READ (1734–1798). A member of the General Assembly of Delaware from 1765 to 1778, he was elected to the Continental Congress from 1774 to 1776, withdrawing in 1777 to spend more time on state issues. He was a delegate to the Constitutional Convention in 1787 and was elected to the U.S. Senate from 1788 to 1793. From 1793 to 1798 he presided as chief justice of the Supreme Court of Delaware.

CAESAR RODNEY (1730–1783). Selected as a delegate to the Stamp Act Congress of 1765, and chosen as speaker of the Provincial Assembly from 1769–1774, he was elected to the Continental Congress from 1774–1778. Appointed brigadier general of his province by Congress, he put down Tory uprisings in Delaware and, after joining Washington's main army when Howe marched on Philadelphia, returned to Delaware to help maintain a state of equilibrium there.

THOMAS McKEAN (1734–1817). A Delaware delegate to the Stamp Act Congress, he was elected to the General Congress of 1774 and remained a member of the Continental Congress until the peace treaty of 1783. He wrote the Delaware Constitution in 1776. Claimed by both Delaware and Pennsylvania, he was Chief Justice of Pennsylvania from 1779 to 1799, then Governor from 1800 to 1808.

THOMAS STONE (1743–1787). A Maryland delegate to the first Continental Congress in 1774, he later worked on the committee that framed the Articles of Confederation in 1777, and resigned from Congress in 1778 to labor for their adoption in the state legislature. He returned to Congress in 1783, was present when General Washington resigned his military commission, and in 1784 served as president of Congress.

SAMUEL CHASE (1741–1811). One of five Maryland delegates to the first Continental Congress in 1774, Chase remained in Congress until 1778. He was appointed chief justice of the Maryland Supreme Court in 1788, and was nominated to the United States Supreme Court by President Washington in 1796. He served as a Supreme Court justice for 15 years.

WILLIAM PACA (1740–1799). Paca was a member of the Continental Congress from 1774–1778, when he was appointed chief justice of the Maryland Supreme Court. In 1782 he was elected governor of Maryland, then retired after one term. A member of the Maryland convention to ratify the U.S. Constitution in 1788, his efforts led President Washington to name him a U.S. district judge for Maryland in 1789.

CHARLES CARROLL (1737–1832). A fierce advocate of independence, he fought members of his own state legislature to have freedom proclaimed and was elected to the Continental Congress only in 1776, too late to vote *Charles Carroll of Carrollton* for approval of the Declaration— but not too late to sign. He remained politically active until 1801 and outlived all the other signers of the Declaration.

VIRGINIA

RICHARD HENRY LEE (1732–1794). Elected to the Virginia House of Burgesses at age 25, he was the first Virginian publicly to oppose the Stamp Act. A delegate to the General Congress, he introduced the resolution for total separation from England on June 7, 1776. A member *Richard Henry Lee* of Congress until 1779, and again from 1784 to 1789, he was the first U.S. senator from Virginia under the new Constitution, which he had opposed.

GEORGE WYTHE (1726–1806). A member of the Virginia House of Burgesses, he was elected to the General Congress in 1775, and in 1776 he was chosen speaker of the House of Burgesses. He was a judge in the Virginia high court of Chancery, 1778–86. A Virginia delegate to the Constitutional Convention and twice elected to the U.S. Senate, he freed all his adult slaves during his lifetime.

BENJAMIN HARRISON (1726?–1791).
Elected to the Virginia House of Burgesses at a young age, he soon became speaker. A delegate to the first Continental Congress in 1774, he remained in Congress until 1777. He was a member of the Virginia legislature and speaker, 1777–82 and 1784–91. Governor of Virginia, 1782-84, he was the father of President William Henry Harrison, great-grandfather of Benjamin.

THOMAS JEFFERSON (1743–1826). He was elected to the Virginia legislature in 1769, and to the Continental Congress in 1775. He chaired the committee to draft the Declaration and wrote the first draft. In 1779 he succeeded Patrick Henry as governor of Virginia. Washington's first secretary of state, vice president under John Adams, and third president of the United States, he was the founder and rector of the University of Virginia. Jefferson's library, purchased by Congress for $30,000 in 1815, became the first component of the Library of Congress. He died on July 4, 1826.

CARTER BRAXTON (1736–1797). He became a member of the Virginia House of Burgesses in 1765 and was elected to the Continental Congress in 1774. He returned to the Virginia legislature in 1776, continuing there until 1785. He was appointed to the state council, 1786–91, and again 1794–97.

THOMAS NELSON JR. (1738–1789). Elected to the Virginia House of Burgesses in 1774, he was elected to the General Congress that same year. The first to propose a state militia to defend the rights of the people, he was appointed commander-in-chief of the state forces in 1777, and used his own resources to recruit troops. He succeeded Jefferson as governor in 1781 but retained command of his troops, and took part in the battle of Yorktown and the capture of Cornwallis in 1781.

FRANCIS LIGHTFOOT LEE (1734–1797). A member of the Virginia legislature from 1765 to 1775, Lee was elected to the Continental Congress in 1775. He served in Congress until 1779, and was on the committee that framed the Articles of Confederation. He was elected to the Virginia Senate in 1779, but retired after one session.

NORTH CAROLINA

JOSEPH HEWES (1730–1779). He moved to North Carolina from New Jersey in 1760 and was elected to the legislature in 1763. A delegate to the General Congress of 1774, he was elected again in 1775 and, as head of the naval committee, was in effect the first secretary of the navy. Soon after signing the Declaration in 1776 he left to tend to his business, but he returned to Congress in 1779 and died in Philadelphia.

WILLIAM HOOPER (1742–1790). He studied law under James Otis before moving to North Carolina. Elected to the Provincial Assembly in 1773, and appointed as the state's first delegate to the Continental Congress in 1774, he began agitating for complete separation from England as early as 1775. He remained in Congress until 1777, then returned to North Carolina to protect his home and family.

JOHN PENN (1741–1788). Largely self-taught, he was admitted to the bar in Virginia at 21. He moved to North Carolina in 1774 and was elected a delegate to the Continental Congress in 1775. In 1780 he was authorized by the state legislature to organize the defense of the western part of the state against Cornwallis's army, invading from the south. He and his patriot bands harrassed the British troops and kept them out of Virginia.

EDWARD RUTLEDGE (1749–1800). A delegate from South Carolina at the first General Congress in 1774, he was reelected in 1775, 1776 and 1779. He returned to South Carolina to help defend the state and was taken prisoner in 1780 during the siege of Charleston and shipped to St. Augustine. Exchanged after a year, he was active in the state legislature until elected to the U.S. Senate in 1794.

THOMAS HEYWARD, JR. (1746–1809). Involved in the patriot cause after the Stamp Act of 1765, he was chosen a delegate from South Carolina to the General Congress in 1775, and remained in Congress until 1778. In 1778 he was appointed a judge in South Carolina and sat on the bench until 1798. Commissioned during the Revolutionary War, he was wounded, then later captured and sent to St. Augustine for a year.

THOMAS LYNCH, JR. (1749–1779). In 1776 Lynch was elected to replace his ailing father as a South Carolina delegate to the Continental Congress. After signing the Declaration, he resigned to escort his father home, but the old man died in Annapolis. Ill himself, the son and his young wife embarked for the south of Europe to recuperate, but their ship disappeared at sea.

ARTHUR MIDDLETON (1743–1788). Elected a delegate to the General Congress in 1776, he remained in Congress until 1777. He joined in the defense of South Carolina, had his estate ravaged by the British in 1779, and was taken prisoner in 1780 and sent to St. Augustine. Exchanged after a year, he was elected to Congress, then left in 1782 and was a representative in the state legislature until late 1787.

BUTTON GWINNETT (1732–1777). Born in England, in 1770 he emigrated to Charleston, then moved to Georgia in 1772. At first opposed to a break with England, he joined the cause in 1775 and was elected to the Continental Congress in 1775. He remained in Congress until 1777, when he joined the state convention to write a Constitution. He was elected president of the council, but lost his life in a duel that same year.

LYMAN HALL (1721–1784). A doctor, he emigrated to Georgia from New England and was instrumental in getting that state to join the cause of freedom. Delegated to the General Congress in 1775 as an independent, then elected one of five delegates from Georgia in 1776, he remained in Congress until 1780. The British confiscated his property, but in 1782 he returned to Georgia and in 1783 was elected governor.

GEORGE WALTON (1740–1804). He moved to Georgia from Virginia, but did not begin practicing law until 1774. Appointed one of five delegates to the Continental Congress in 1776, Walton remained in Congress until 1778, when he returned home to help defend the state as colonel of a regiment. Wounded and captured in the war, he later served as governor, congressman, U.S. senator, and chief justice of Georgia.

In CONGRESS. July 4, 1776.

The unanimous Declaration of the thirteen united States of America.